ANIMAL HEROES

SUPERMOMS!

IT'S SUPERMOM!

No, it's a plane.

HEATHER LANG and **JAMIE HARPER**

illustrated by **JAMIE HARPER**

CANDLEWICK PRESS

Supermoms are everywhere. They come in all shapes, sizes, colors, and species. With powerful instincts and extraordinary skills, these moms do whatever it takes to protect and raise their young.

Some supermoms are pros at making safe and comfy homes.

A groundhog mom builds a five-star burrow, including a bathroom and a nursery lined with soft grasses for her pups.

Danger lurks outside, so a red-knobbed hornbill mom seals the entrance to her nest with mud and poop. She keeps her eggs and, later, her chicks safe inside for three months.

A strawberry poison frog mom puts each youngster in its own private pool . . . to keep her tadpoles from killing one another.

Supermoms make enormous sacrifices to feed their young.

To find food, an emperor penguin mom might trek fifty miles (eighty kilometers). She could be gone for two months. With a full belly, she spits up the food to feed her chick.

I'm home!

A polar bear mom never gets a night out. She doesn't leave her den or eat a single bite for up to eight months because she's so busy feeding her cubs.

A bearded capuchin monkey mom is so super, she'll feed and groom an orphan baby, even if it's a different kind of monkey.

Didn't you say you wanted a *little* brother?

RAAAAAH!

I changed my mind.

Supermoms are creative when it comes to transportation.

A wolf spider mom hauls a heavy load—carrying hundreds of spiderlings at once. If danger is near, she signals them to climb on board.

A little brown bat mom carries her pup on her chest . . . while she's flying.

Mom! Mom! Do the dip of death.

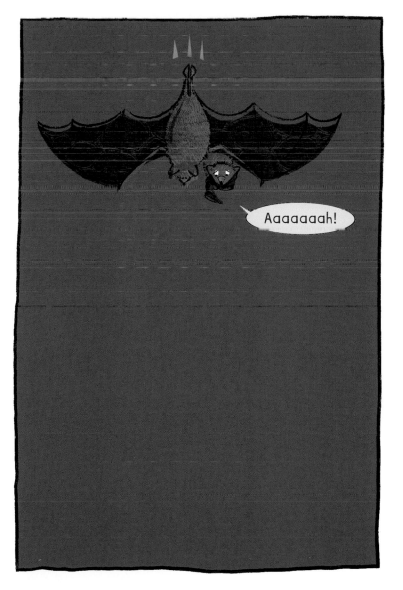

Aaaaaaah!

Supermoms stop at nothing to protect their young.

White-spotted cichlid youngsters are a tasty treat for lots of fish.
Mom sucks them into her mouth to save them from danger.

A giant Pacific octopus mom cleans and guards thousands of eggs for five months or more until they hatch. She never leaves them alone.

A cheetah mom always stays one step ahead of danger. She moves her cubs every few days to make sure predators won't pick up their scent.

An elephant calf doesn't have just one supermom to keep him safe—he has a whole herd of females, called allomothers.

Poor guy...

BUMS TOGETHER, LADIES!

A piping plover mom lures predators away from her chicks . . .

by pretending to have a broken wing.

A bottlenose dolphin mom shows her calf how to safely forage for food on the rough ocean floor by using sea sponges to protect their beaks.

An orangutan is one super-duper mom. She devotes eight years to teaching her baby how to find food . . .

use tools . . .

and weave sleeping mats in the treetops.

Is it over-under or under-over?

Supermoms are everywhere. They come in all shapes, sizes, colors, and species.

With powerful instincts and extraordinary skills, these moms give their youngsters everything they need to go out into the world and thrive.

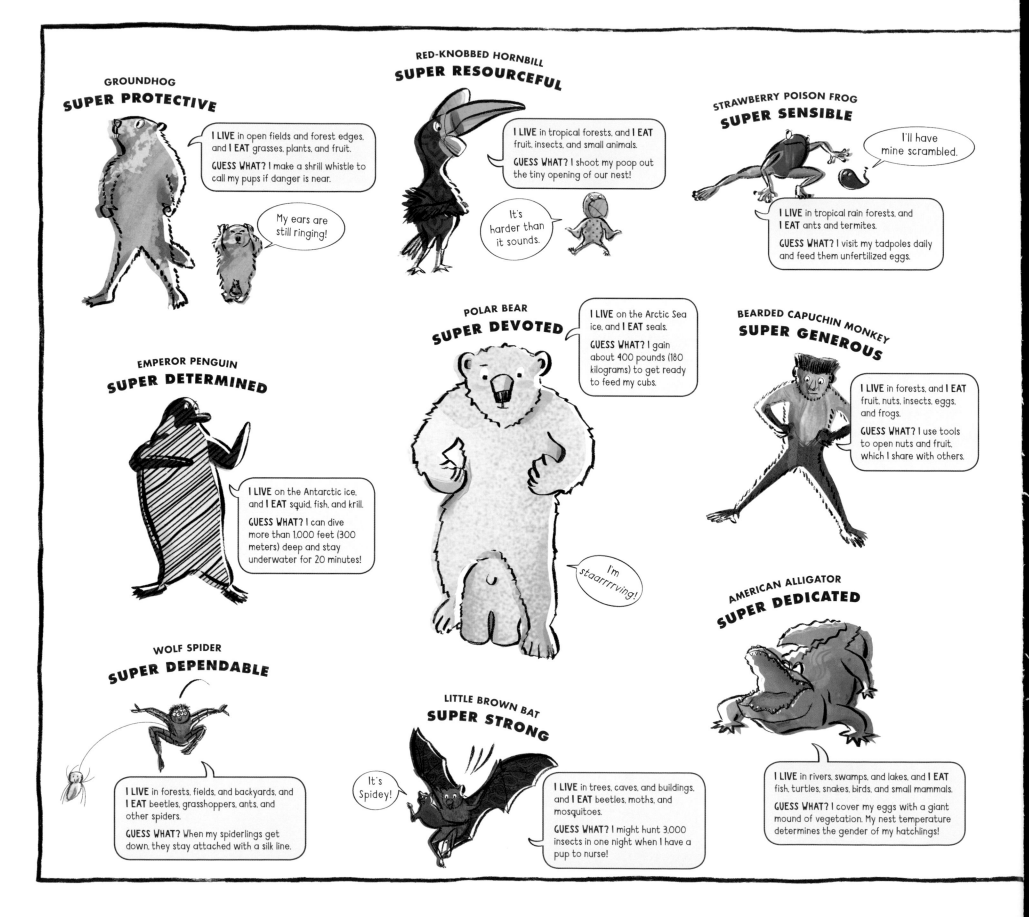

Dive in to learn more!

CHILDREN'S BOOKS

Davies, Nicola. *Dolphin Baby!* Illustrated by Brita Granström. Somerville, MA: Candlewick, 2012.

Desmond, Jenni. *The Elephant.* Brooklyn, NY: Enchanted Lion Books, 2018.

Guiberson, Brenda. *Ice Bears.* Illustrated by Ilya Spirin. New York: Henry Holt, 2008.

Jenkins, Steve, and Robin Page. *The Frog Book.* New York: Houghton Mifflin Harcourt, 2019.

London, Jonathan. *Otters Love to Play.* Illustrated by Meilo So. Somerville, MA: Candlewick, 2018.

Markle, Sandra. *A Mother's Journey.* Illustrated by Alan Marks. Watertown, MA: Charlesbridge, 2006.

——. *Wolf Spiders: Mothers on Guard.* Minneapolis: Lerner, 2011.

Marsh, Laura. *Cheetahs.* Washington, DC: National Geographic Kids, 2019.

——. *Giraffes.* Washington, DC: National Geographic Kids, 2016.

Pringle, Laurence. *The Secret Life of the Little Brown Bat.* Illustrated by Kate Garchinsky. Honesdale, PA: Boyds Mills Press, 2018.

Wallace, Karen. *Gentle Giant Octopus.* Illustrated by Mike Bostock. Somerville, MA: Candlewick, 2002.

ONLINE RESOURCES

"About Bats." Bat Conservation International. https://www.batcon.org/about-bats.

"American Alligator." San Diego Zoo. https://kids.sandiegozoo.org/animals/american-alligator.

Cheetah Conservation Fund. https://cheetah.org/.

"Emperor Penguin: The Majestic Bird of Antarctica." aboutanimals: The Online Animal Encyclopedia. https://www.aboutanimals.com/bird/emperor-penguin/.

"Hornbill." San Diego Zoo Wildlife Alliance Animals & Plants. https://animals.sandiegozoo.org/animals/hornbill.

"Orangutans." Orangutan Foundation International. https://orangutan.org.orangutan-facts/.

"Poison Frog." San Diego Zoo Wildlife Alliance Animals & Plants. https://animals.sandiegozoo.org/animals/poison-frog.

"Polar Bears." SeaWorld Parks & Entertainment. https://seaworld.org/animals/all-about/polar-bear/.

AUDIOVISUAL RESOURCES

Animal Super Parents. Directed by Christina Nutter. BBC, 2015.

Arctic Tale. Directed by Adam Ravetch and Sarah Robertson. National Geographic, 2007.

Born to Be Wild. Directed by David Lickley. IMAX Corporation, 2011.

"Bringing Up Baby: The Natural History of a Mother's Love." Season 28, episode 5, of *Natural World.* Produced by Mark Fletcher. BBC, 2009.

Dolphin Reef. Produced by Keith Scholey and Alastair Fothergill. Disneynature, 2018.

Growing Up Wild. Directed by Mark Linfield and Keith Scholey. Disneynature, 2016.

March of the Penguins. Directed by Luc Jacquet. National Geographic Films, 2005.

AUTHORS' WEBSITES

Visit heatherlangbooks.com and jamieharper.com for additional resources and activities, including links to videos of supermoms in action and information about other sources we used to research this book.

ACKNOWLEDGMENTS

We are grateful to the following experts for helping us verify facts and gain new insights into supermoms: SeaWorld Education and Conservation Department's Ask Shamu team; Lorna Blocksma, supervisor of visitor experience at the New England Aquarium; Dr. Matthew B. Dugas, assistant professor, Illinois State University; Andrew Furness, evolutionary biologist, University of Hull; Ad Konings, Cichlid Press; Bob Lee, animal curator and elephant manager at the Oregon Zoo; Brian D. Linkhart, professor, Department of Organismal Biology and Ecology at Colorado College; Puja Pawar, wildlife biologist, Centre for Cellular and Molecular Biology, India; Dr. Jennifer L. Stynoski, research professor, Institute Clodomiro Picado at the University of Costa Rica; and George W. Uetz, professor of biological sciences at the University of Cincinnati.

For Lyda, my longtime super friend,
who's also a SUPERMOM
HL

For Lucy, Georgia, and Grace,
who make being a mom a true joy
JH

First edition 2023

Library of Congress Catalog Card Number 2022907034
ISBN 978-1-5362-1797-1

22 23 24 25 26 27 CCP 10 9 8 7 6 5 4 3 2 1

Printed in Shenzhen, Guangdong, China

This book was typeset in Futura.
The illustrations were done using traditional and digital collage.

Candlewick Press
99 Dover Street
Somerville, Massachusetts 02144

www.candlewick.com